ÒGÚN

IFÁ AND THE SPIRIT OF IRON

AWO FÁ'LOKUN FATUNMBI
OMO AWO FATUNMISE, ILẸ́ IFẸ,
BABALAWO ÈGBÈ IFÁ, ODẸ RẸMO,
OLÚWO ILẸ́ ÒRÚNMÌLÁ OSHUN, OAKLAND, CA

ÒGÚN

IFÁ AND THE SPIRIT OF IRON
Awo Fá'lókun Fátunmbi

ISBN: 0-942272-28-5

Cover illustration by *Awo Fá'lókun Fátunmbi*
Printed in the United States of America

Original Publications
P.O. BOX 236
Old Bethpage, New York 11804-0236
1 (888) OCCULT - 1

ACKNOWLEDGEMENTS

The material in this book is primarily based on oral instruction from the elders of *Ifá* in Odẹ Remo, Ogun State Nigeria and Ilẹ́ Ifẹ, Oshun State Nigeria. In appreciation for their time, patience and loving concern for my training and spiritual guidance I say; *A dúpé Ègbè Ifá Ode Remo, Babalawo* Adesanya Awoyade, *Babalawo* Babalola Akinsanya, *Babalawo* Saibu Lamiyo, *Babalawo* Odujosi Awoyade, *Babalawo* Olu Taylor, *Babalawo* Abokede Aralbadan, *Babalawo* Biodun Debona, *Babalawo* Oluwasina Kuti, *Babalawo* Afolabi Kuti, *Babalawo* Fagbemi Fasina, *Babalawo* Oropotoniyan and all the members of Ègbè Apetebi Ode Remo.

A dúpé Awon Ifá Fatunmise Ègbè Ifá Ilẹ́ Ifé, Jolofinpe Falaju Fatunmise, *Babalawo* Ganiyu Olaifa Fatunmise, *Babalawo* Awoleke Awofisan Lokore, *Babalawo* Ifaioye Fatunmise, *Babalawo* Ifanimowu Fatunmise, *Babalawo* Ifasure Fatunmise *Babalawo* Adebolu Fatunmise and all the members of *Egbe Apetebi Awon Fatunmise.*

A special thank you to the members of *Ilé Òrúnmìlà Oshun* for their continuing support and understanding, *Olori Yeye Aworo Timi Lade, Apetebi Orunmila, Iya l'Orisha Oshun Miwa* (Luisah Teish), *Eko'fa Iya l'Orisha Omijinka, Iya l'Orisha Iya Oshun Iya Osogbo, Iya l'Orisha Shango Wenwa,* Leona Jacobs-White, Nzinga Denny, Earthea Nance, Vance Williams, Blackberri, Salim Abdul-Jelani, Rebecca Schiros, Carol Lanigan, Zena Attig, T'hisha, Rose Sand, Xochipala Maes Valdez, Dee Orr, Nina Heft and Jemoke.

A final thank you to Maureen Pattarelli for her work in editing this manuscript.

A dúpé okuku su wi awo aganjo, I thank all those who greet the Mysteries of Creation.

Awo Fá'lokun Fatunmbi
Oakland, CA

TABLE OF CONTENTS

INTRODUCTION

Ògún is the Spirit of Iron in the West African religious tradition called *Ifá*. The word *Ògún* is the name given to describe a complex convergence of Spiritual Forces that are key elements in *Ifá* cosmology. There is no literal translation for the word *Ifá*, it refers to a religious tradition, an understanding of ethics, a process of spiritual transformation and a set of scriptures that are the basis for a complex system of divination.

Ifá is found throughout the African diaspora where it spread as an integral part of Yoruba culture. The Yoruba Nation is located in the Southwestern region of Nigeria. Prior to colonization, the Yoruba Nation was a federation of city states that was originally centered in the city of *Ilé Ifè*. According to *Ifá* myth, the Yorubas migrated to *Ilé Ifè* from the east under the leadership of a warrior chief named *Oduduwa*. It is difficult to date the time of the Yoruba move into West Africa because of limited archaeological research on the subject. Estimates range from between sixteen hundred to twenty-five hundred years ago. It is likely that migration took place over a number of generations. As the population grew, each new city state that became a part of the Yoruba federation was governed by a chief called "*Qba*". The position of *Qba* is a form of hereditary monarchy and each *Qba* goes through an initiation that makes them a spiritual descendant of *Oduduwa*.

Traditional Yoruba political institutions are very much integrated with traditional Yoruba religious institutions. Both structures survived British rule in Nigeria, and continue to function alongside the current civil government.

Within the discipline of *Ifá*, there is a body of wisdom called "*awo*", which attempts to preserve the rituals that create direct communication with Forces in Nature. *Awo* is a Yoruba word that is usually translated to mean "secret". Unfortunately, there is no real English equivalent to the word *awo*, because the word carries strong cultural and esoteric associations. In traditional Yoruba culture, *awo* refers to the hidden principles that explain the Mystery of Creation and Evolution. *Awo* is the esoteric understanding of the invisible forces that sustain dynamics and form within Nature. The essence of these invisible forces are not considered secret because they are devious, they are secret because they remain elusive, awesome in their power to transform and not readily apparent. As such they can only be grasped through direct interaction and participation. Anything which can be known by the intellect alone ceases to be *awo*.

The primal inspiration for *awo* is the communication between transcendent Spiritual Forces and human consciousness. This communication is believed to be facilitated by the Spirit of *Eṣu* who is the Divine Messenger. Working in close association with *Eṣu* is *Ògún* who has the power to clear away those obstacles that stand in the way of spiritual growth. *Ògún* is also the primal source of the *aṣẹ* (power) that sustains Creation.

The essence of *Ògún* is considered one of many Spiritual Forces in Nature which are called *Orisha*. The word *Orisha* means "Select Head". In a cultural context, *Orisha* is a reference to the various Forces in Nature that guide consciousness. According to *Ifá*, everything in Nature has some form of consciousness canned "*Orí*". The *Orí* of all animals, plants and humans is believed to be guided by a specific Force in Nature (*Orisha*) which defines the quality of a particular form of consciousness. There are a large number of *Orisha* and each *Orisha* has its own *awo*.

The unique function of *Ògún* within the realm of *Orisha Awo* (Mysteries of Nature) is to remove all obstacles that stand in the way of spiritual evolution, which includes the evolution of all that is. In order to do this *Ògún* must sacrifice all that stands in the way of spiritual evolution. Because of these sacred responsibility *Ògún* is considered the Guardian of Truth. *Ògún* does not protect the truth of what we would like to be, he guards the truth of what is. It is the process of making this distinction that lies at the core of *Ògún's* mystery.

I.

ALQ IRITÀN ÒGÚN
FOLKTALES OF THE SPIRIT OF IRON

A. *ÒGÚN ADÉ* — The Crown of the Spirit of Iron

In the olden days, *Ororinna* married *Tabutu*. Together they had a son who was known as *Tobi Odę* (the skilled hunter). It was *Tobi Odę* (the skilled hunter) who became first among the *Orisha* (Immortals) to make the Journey from *Ikolę Ọrun* (the Invisible Realm) to *Ikolę Ayę (Earth)*. The *Orisha* (the Immortals) who followed discovered that *Ikolę Ayę* (Earth) was covered with *igbo* (dense forest) that made it impossible to travel across the land.

Obatala The Chief of the White Cloth) decided that he would make a path through the forest. He took his *àdá fadákà* (silver cutlass) and slashed at the underbrush. The *àdá fadákà* (silver cutlass) became bent and twisted and was useless for the task of clearing the forest.

Tobi Odę (the skilled hunter) discovered the *awo* (mystery) of *irin* (iron) and made *àdá irin* (iron cutlass). The *àdá irin* (iron cutlass) cut a clear path through the forest and the *Orisha* (the Immortals) were able to make the journey across *aiyę* (the land). It was on that day that *Tobi Odę* (the skilled hunter) became known as *Ògún* (the Spirit of Iron).

The *Orisha* (the Immortals) were so impressed with the strength of *àdá irin* (iron cutlass) that they gave *Ògún* the title of "*Osin Imolę*", which means "First among the Immortals". *Ògún* was unimpressed with his status as *Olori* (chief) of *Ilę Ifę* (spreading earth) because he preferred living alone in *igbo* (the forest). Using his *àdá irin* (iron cutlass), *Ògún* cut a path that lead all the way to *okę giga* (the mountains). Living in the high ground, *Ògún* was able to hunt and fish and lead a life of contentment.

On the day that *Ògún* decided to visit his friends in *Ilę Ifę* (spreading earth), he started down the long path that lead from *okę giga* (the mountain) to *afonífojì* (the valley). The living in *igbo* (the forest), *Ògún* made clothes from *mariwo* (palm fronds), which gave him the appearance of a wild man. As he reached the bottom of the trail, he was tired from the rugged journey and there was a frown on his face.

The first town that he approached was called *Ire* (good fortune) on the outskirts of *Ekiti* (the mound). While resting in *Ire* (good fortune), *Ògún* helped the people of the village defeat their enemies. From that day on he has been known as "*Onire*", which means "The Chief of Good Fortune".

Ògún decided to continue his journey to *Ilę Ifę* (spreading earth) still covered with the blood of battle. When he arrived at the sacred city, the people of *Ilę Ifę* were frightened by the sight of the wild man dressed in *mariwo* (palm fronds) who carried the scars of war. They pleaded with him to go away. Instead, *Ògún* washed himself and appeared in the center of town as *Osin Imolę* (First Among the Immortals). When the people of *Ilę Ifę* realized that the wild man they had scorned was their chief, they begged for his forgiveness and asked him to stay.

Ògún refused their request, saying that he no longer wanted to be first among the *Orisha* (The Immortals). On that day *Ògún* returned to *igbo* (the forest), where he lives to this day, dancing among the trees. This is why those who worship *Ògún* (*the Spirit of Iron*) say, "*Da fun Ògún awo, ni jo ti ma lana lati odę, Ògún wa si is salu aiyę, fun ire ida,*" which means, "The Spirit of Iron gives you his secret, dancing outside opens the road, The Invisible Realm comes to Earth for the benefit of all the people."

Commentary: In many of the books written about *Orisha*, *Ògún* is described as a "bloodthirsty warrior" who constantly invokes destruction and violence. This description owes more to the stereotypical images of the African hunter than it does to the deep metaphysical principles represented by the Spirit of *Ògún*.

For many people who live in an urban environment the concept of hunting is limited to the idea of killing game for sport. This is not an idea expressed in Yoruba culture, where hunting remains an important component of the survival needs of the community. Yoruba society is primarily based upon farming. It is the task of the rural hunter to provide sources of food that do not come from either planted crops or domesticated livestock. Because the hunter must move and work within the dense jungle of the rainforest, the community depends on the hunters to locate medicinal herbs, to warn of potential hazards to the village, and to provide those sources of food that give variety and balance to the overall diet. Given this range of responsibilities, the role of the hunter remains an honorable, respected and spiritually elevated task within traditional Yoruba society.

The myth of *Ògún* presents both metaphysical information and a historical account of the shifting role of the hunter in Yoruba culture. In all parts of the world the earliest manifestations of culture were centered around extended families that were set up as hunting and gathering clans. The early hunters were the skilled technicians of their day. The technology of the hunt was considered a sacred mystery which gave most hunters the dual role of tracker and shaman. It was the improvement of the tools used in the hunt that lead to the development of those tools which lead to farming. The tools developed for farming in turn lead to the development of those tools used to create cities and modern civilization as we know it today. In some ways the Spirit of Iron represents the fusion between the Laws of Nature and the human effort to apply those Laws to the demands of survival.

In the myth of *Ògún*, the silver cutlass of *Obatala* is ineffective for the rigors of clearing a path through the forest. The silver cutlass is a symbolic image for the power of thought and contemplation. Building civilizations as a historical process required more than the use of rational solutions applied to improving standards of living. Real development in the area of culture and technology required hands-on-experience, trial and error, exploration of the unknown, and the relentless search for real solutions to life threaten-

ing problems. In *Ifá*, the image used to describe this slow process
of cultural transformation is the tempering of iron.

When the use of iron was first developed to improve the quality
of tools, the technology of forging metal was considered a highly
secret, esoteric art that was only shared among those who showed
signs of good character, perseverance and intelligence. As in the
myth of *Ògún*, those who possessed the knowledge of the mystery
of iron were placed in positions of responsibility as priests and
chiefs. With the growth of civilization, it became necessary to
explore new vistas of achievement such as architecture, medicine
and farming. This shift in emphasis caused a diminishment in the
respect given to those who maintained the skills of the hunter and
the blacksmith.

The myth of *Ògún* reflects this historical shift by showing
Ògún coming down off the mountain in the clothes of a wild
man. As the demands of city life took culture further and further
away from the need to depend on hunting and gathering, the skills
and courage needed for the hunt became suppressed. In the myth,
the people of *Ilẹ̀ Ifẹ* are frightened by *Ògún* when he returns
home after the battle in *Ire*. *Ògún* is so disgusted by their fear
that he returns to the forest where he reclaims his childhood
reputation as a skilled hunter.

In traditional Yoruba culture it is the initiates of *Ògún* who
still maintain the *awo* for making tools, who still hunt for food,
and who have a key role in maintaining the security of the village.
None of these tasks are viewed in Yoruba society as "bloodthirsty,"
or "savage." Instead, they are considered an essential element in
the overall balance and harmony of the community as a whole.
Because these roles are viewed as important and necessary, they
are given religious sanction through initiation and priestly responsibility.

It is the initiates of *Ògún* who lead male puberty rites, who
perform the rite of circumcision, and who take an active role in the
ceremonial preparation of food from both domesticated animals and
wildlife from the forest. Despite the negative images of "animal
sacrifice" that frequently appear in movies and on television, the
role of those who prepare meat for human consumption are believed

to be performing a sacred rite. *"Obẹ,"* which means "knife" is sacred to *Ògún*. Every time an animal is slaughtered for use as food, an offering is made to *Orisha*, even if the offering is only to the knife itself.

In *Ifá*, the presentation of animal blood to *Orisha* is called *"ebo,"* which means "life force offering." This offering is considered a covenant between humans and *Orisha*. The covenant is both a prayer of gratitude for the blessings of nourishment, and a prayer of respect for those Forces in Nature that continue to provide food for the health and well being of the community. *Ifá* teaches that all life comes from a single rock called *"Oyigiyigi."* Generally, the life force offering is given to some type of consecrated rock as a symbol of the metaphysical principle that all life returns to Source.

The idea that such a covenant represents some form of "bloodthirsty" and "destructive" behavior is not a part of *Ifá* cosmology and is inconsistent with the cultural perception of the process. *Ògún* is more accurately seen as the great provider, the guardian of truth about the dynamics of balance in Nature, and the guide for those who must transform their consciousness from the realities of childhood to the responsibilities of becoming an adult.

There is an element of aggressive behavior in *Ògún's* roles as warrior or guardian of family, village and nation. In this Myth, *Ògún* rejects the title of Chief and returns to the forest where he can sharpen his skills as a warrior. This abandonment of the throne represents the historical shift in Yoruba culture between those political leaders who were primarily military strategists, and those political leaders who aspired to maintain the ethical standards of *Ifá* as expressed through the ethical teachings of the prophet *Ọrúmìlà*. This does not suggest that *Ògún's* role is any less sacred. It merely points to a shift in the skills needed to effectively govern the nation as culture evolved.

In metaphysical terms, *Ògún* represents the power of the Spirit of Evolution to mold new life forms and new structures within the overall unfolding of Creation. It is in this role, as a fundamental Force of Natural Law, that *Ògún* is used as a symbol for Truth. All oaths taken within the context of both *Ifá* and *Orisha*

worship are sworn on the sacred religious depositories of Ògún's
aṣẹ (spiritual power).

Traditionally the vessels of Ògún's aṣẹ are made from iron.
In Nature iron is produced by the cooling of molten minerals at the
core of the Earth. When iron first poured into the ocean floor from
the center of the Earth, it formed iron deposits which created rust.
Some Western scientists believe that the bacteria which developed
from the rust was the seed that generated the first life forms on the
planet. Ifá describes this process as the virility of Ògún's aṣẹ.

B. ÒGÚN WA'LẸ ONIRE — The Spirit of Iron Comes to the Village of Onire

Ògún (the Spirit of Iron) was resting in the mountains when
he heard yelling and screaming from the valley below. He picked
up both of his àdá (cutlasses) and ran down the mountain. As he
approached the village of Onire, Ògún could see that it was under
attack.

With an àdá (cutlass) in each hand, Ògún came charging
down the mountain. Ògún raised the àdá (cutlasses) above his
head and said, "Ẹ́mi liege, ẹ́mi si lajabo, mo lafeeeri pẹlu, mo
layẹta odẹ." (I have the medicine of a warrior, I have the medicine
of a hunter).

Ògún was wearing moriwo l'aso Ògún (a red cloth and
palm fronds), and as he moved into ìjá (battle) the moriwo (palm
fronds) turned blood red. When there was no one left to challenge
his àdá (cutlass), Ògún said, "Ko si 'gba ta o ni ku." (Death is
the inevitable fate of all humans).

Having defended the village of Onire from destruction, Ògún
walked to the well for a drink of water. As the people of Onire saw
him walk through the streets of their village they pleaded with him
to leave. In a rage, Ògún raised his àdá, and the water from the
well turned red.

When he realized that he had killed the people of his own
village, Ògún felt ashamed and went to live in a hole in the
ground. As he made his way into the Earth, he left a chain dangling

from the hole and told the people of *Onire* that they could summon him by pulling the chain.

That is why those who worship *Ògún* (the Spirit of Iron) say, "*Ìrèmọjẹ́ Ògún lodẹ fi i saaro ara won, keni o gbon rohun mu dira.*" (The hunters chant the praise of the Spirit of Iron to mourn his death and the wise gain inspiration from his deeds)

Commentary: The worship of *Ògún* in Africa is closely associated with the craft of the blacksmith. However, *Ògún* is also worshipped by both warriors and hunters. In pre-colonial times the society of *Ògún* worshipers, (*ẹ̀gbẹ̀ Ògún*) in conjunction with certain ancestral societies, (*ẹ̀gbẹ̀ isẹgun*) had a primary role in the protection of the community.

In most cultures the art of warfare is associated with powers of "male aggression." In Yoruba the word "*Ìjala*" is used to mean "warrior." It is a contraction of the word "*ìja*," meaning "war" or "fight," and the word "*ala*" meaning "white cloth." The symbol of white cloth is associated with *Obatala*, who is the Chief of the White Cloth. In *Ifá*, one of the functions of *Obatala* is to maintain ethical standards within the culture. The word *ijala* suggests that the essence of the warrior is aligned with moral principles and those ideals that are at the foundation of spiritual transformation.

The myth of *Ògún* at *Onire* shows *Ògún* coming to the defense of his village. Yoruba oral history tells of a large migration of *Ògún* worshippers from the city of *Ilẹ́ Ifẹ* to the city of *Onire* in the formative years of the Yoruba Federation. Once he has successfully ended the siege, *Ògún* comes into the village in search of water. The people of the city are so frightened by his appearance that they ask him to leave. At this point *Ògún's* aggression turns against the people of his own village.

Ifá considers the aggression symbolized by *Ògún's* power as a warrior to be an integral part of the dynamics of Nature. It is linked to the will to survive that exists in all species. Throughout Nature, the large animals eat the smaller animals, the large plants smother the smaller plants, and those animals which are able to defend themselves effectively become stable within a particular ecological niche. As part of the socializing process the aggression associated with the Warrior Spirit remains a necessary aspects of survival.

The socializing process is based on the relationship between *Ògún* and *Obatala*. It is the function of *Obatala* to determine when and how the Warrior Spirit is to manifest. Those *Ìjala* who maintain the discipline of the warrior make use of ritual and invocation to access and suppress the powers represented by *Ògún*. This process is symbolized in the story through the use of the image of *Ògún* entering a hole in the ground. In mythology when something is placed in an opening in the Earth, it is a reference to the power of those traits that are traditional identified as "feminine." This suggests that the dynamic element of *Ògún* is kept in balance by the powers associated with *Onilẹ*, who is the Spirit of the Earth.

In *Ifá*, *Onilẹ* is the Spiritual Force which defines the dynamics of "*onídajọ́*," which means justice, and "*idọgba*" which means "equality." Both *onìdajọ́* and *idọgba* are described by *Ifá* as concepts that can be grasped through an understanding of balance in Nature.

In many of the myths and legends associated with *Orisha*, the *Orisha* are shown as flawed, committing errors in judgment that have tragic consequences. The purpose of these stories is to explain the spiritual reasons behind "*ẹwo*," which means "taboo." In the Myth of *Onire*, *Ògún* makes the fatal mistake of turning his rage against his own community. Misdirected anger is one of the potential dangers that is associated with the process of invoking the *aṣẹ* (power) of any Warrior Spirit. The myth shows *Ògún* imposing his own *ẹwo* (taboo) by secluding himself underground. This taboo suggests that *Ògún* was aware of the potential danger inherent in his *aṣẹ* (power), and that he was willing to take precautions to ensure that it was never misdirected again.

The method used by *Ògún* to make *aṣẹ* (power) accessible is a chain. The image of the chain is associated with the idea of genetic evolution. Nature itself is involved in a process of Spiritual Transformation. The content of *onídajọ́* and *idọgba* are constantly shifting as our collective awareness of evolution comes into greater focus. For example, an issue such as the management of the rain forest was of little interest a generation ago. Today it represents a major concern for those who study the health of the planet.

It is common, in *Orisha* literature written in the West, to portray *Ògún* as a "bloodthirsty killer" who draws blood for pleasure. This characterization is both inaccurate and offensive because it demeans the sacred function of *Ògún* in the over balance of self and world.

Ògún as he is represented in the myth of *Onire* is a controlled Force of Nature which remains accessible to those who know *Awo Ògún*, which is the Mystery of the Power of the Spirit of Iron.

Another common misrepresentation of *Ògún* is that he is a rapist. I suspect that the source of this negative characterization is the result of a misunderstanding of *Ògún's* role in male puberty rites. There are multiple psychological transformations that occur during the ceremonies that are performed for young men in traditional Yoruba culture at the age of puberty. A fundamental transformation is the separation of any sexual attachment a young man may feel for his mother. This sexual attachment is a normal feeling among very young boys, and only leads to emotional difficulties if it is not addressed during the early teen years. It is the failure in Western culture to guide young men through this rite of passage that is responsible for the widespread occurrence of sexual violence in non-traditional societies. The fact that *Ògún* is associated with rape in the West says more about our cultural inability to deal with this issue than it says about the nature of *Orisha*.

II.

ÌMỌ̀ ÒGÚN
THE THEOLOGICAL FUNCTION OF THE SPIRIT OF IRON

A. ÒGÚN ÀYÀNMỌ́-ÌPIN — The Spirit of Iron and the Concept of Destiny

The *Ifá* concept of *"àyànmọ́-ìpin,"* which means "Destiny," is based on the belief that each person chooses their individual destiny before being born into the world. These choices materialize as those components that form human potential. Within the scope of each person's potential there exists parameters of choice that can enhance or inhibit the fullest expression of individual destiny. *Ifá* calls these possibilities *"òna ipin,"* which means "fate lines." Each decision that is made in the course of one life time can effect the range of possibilities that exists in the future, by either limiting or expanding the options for growth.

It is within the context of choice, or what is known in Western philosophical tradition as "free will" that *Eṣu* has an important function. Each moment of existence includes a wide range of possible actions, reactions and interpretations. Those moments which require decisive action are described in *Ifá* scripture as *"òna'padẹ,"* which means "junction in the road." Whenever a person who is trying to build character through the use of *Ifá* spiritual discipline reaches *òna'padẹ*, it is customary to consult *Eṣu* regarding the question of which path will bring blessings from *Orisha*.

Ifá teaches that blessings come to those who make choices that are consistent with their highest destiny. Within Yoruba culture it is understood that an individual's highest destiny is based on those choices that build "ìwa-pèlè," which means "good character."

Once the road of good character has been identified, it is the function of *Ògún* to clear away the obstacles that exist along the path of personal destiny. The role of *Ògún* as a warrior in this context is to do whatever needs to be done to effect spiritual transformation. In *Ifá*, when *Ògún* is invoked to remove obstacles it is understood that those obstacles may be either internal or external. Internal obstacles include fear, self doubt, insecurity, confusion, a lack of understanding, and insufficient experience of improper motivation. External obstacles may include injustice, poverty, oppression, natural disaster, illness and misfortune.

One of the key issues associated with *Ògún* that arises during divination is to identify the source of conflict. It is very common for someone struggling with issues of spiritual growth to blame external sources for what may be an internal problem. When this occurs, the real issue is deflected and attention is given to solutions that are doomed to failure because they ignore the root causes of the difficulty in question.

B. *ÒGÚN ONITOJU AŞĘ* — The Spirit of Iron as the Source of Strength

Ifá cosmology is based on the belief that the Primal Source of Creation is a form of Spiritual Essence called "aşę." There is no literal translation for *aşę*, although it is used in prayer to mean "May it be so."

Ifá teaches that the visible universe is generated by two dynamic forces. One is the force of "*inàla*," which means "expansion," and the other is the force of "*isokì*," which means "contraction." The first initial manifestation of these forces is through "ìmo," which means "light," and through "*aimoyé*, which means "darkness." In *Ifá* myth expansion and light are identified with Male Spirits called "*Orisha'ko*." Contraction and darkness are identified with Female Spirits called "*Orisha'bo*." Neither manifestation of *aşę* is considered superior to the other and both are viewed as essential elements in the overall balance of Nature.

In *Ifá* cosmology both *ìmo* and *aimoyę* arise from the matrix of the invisible universe which is called *imolę*, meaning "house of light." Within the house of light there is an invisible substance that transforms spiritual potential into physical reality. The invisible substance that moves between these two dimensions is called *aşę*, and it is *Eşu* who is given the task of guiding the distribution of *aşę* throughout Creation.

When this distribution occurs, the nature of *aşę* takes on different aspects and each of these aspects is commonly associated with a particular Force in Nature called *Orisha*. The word "*Orisha*" means "select head." This is a reference to the belief in *Ifá* that all things which exist in Nature have some form of consciousness. The reference to select head, or *Orisha*, is a reference to the quality of consciousness that guides a particular manifestation of power.

Ògún is that quality of consciousness which can be described in psychological terms as the determined introvert. The person who is willing to do whatever needs to be done to accomplish a task with single minded determination. Elders of *Ògún* in Africa project a quiet determination that reflects a deep inner certainty and inner discipline.

In *Ifá*, *Ògún* is invoked whenever these is a need to make *ebo*, which is a life force offering. In the West, the association between *Ògún* and the ritual offering of animal blood has lead to the mistaken impression that *Ògún* enjoys taking life. This is a gross misrepresentation of *Ògún* ritual function. Whenever animal's are slaughtered for food in traditional Yoruba culture, a portion of the animal's blood is given as an offering. This offering is an on going affirmation of the covenant between humans and Creation Itself. *Ifá* teaches that the universe evolved from a single rock called "*Oyigiyigi*." In turn rocks are placed in sacred shrines as a symbol of the rock from which all Creation emerged. Placing blood on a rock is a ceremonial expression of the metaphysical idea that all things in Creation return to their Source. It is also an offering of thanks to the universe for providing that which sustains human life on Earth.

Part of the discipline of *Ògún* worship is to learn to make the life force offering in a centered and dispassionate way. It is only from this frame of reference that the *Ògún* initiate can effectively elevate the spirit of the animal. The rite of animal spirit elevation is performed so that the "*èmi*," (soul) of the animal will return to Earth to once again provide food for the community.

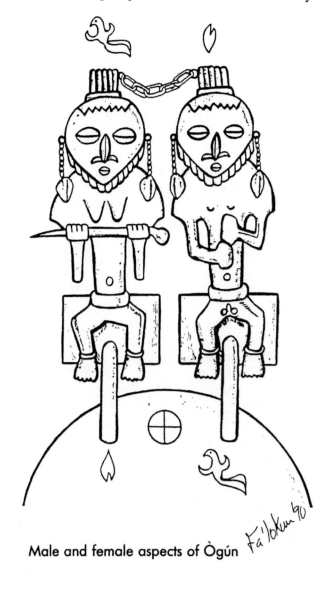

Male and female aspects of Ògún

III.

ÒNA ÒGÚN
THE ROADS OF THE SPIRIT OF IRON

Most *Orisha* worshipping communities in the West tend to recognize *Ògún* in his fundamental manifestation, with little emphasis on his different aspects. In Africa there is some regional variation on the aspects of *Ògún* which are revered as part of community worship. This is a complex subject, but in simple terms there are four aspects of *Ògún* that relate to crafts guilds, and four aspects of *Ògún* that relate to historical figures.

The four aspects of *Ògún* which are related to crafts guilds are: "*Ògún Alágbède*," which is the Spirit of Iron as Guardian of Blacksmiths; "*Ògún-un*," which is the Spirit of Iron as Guardian of Woodcarvers; "*Ògún onigbajamo*," which is the Spirit of Iron as Guardian of Barbers, and "*Ògún Oloola*," which is the Spirit of Iron as Guardian of those who perform circumcisions during male rites of passage.

The five most well-known historical manifestations of *Ògún* are *Ògún Alárá*, which is the Spirit of Iron who was the Chief of Alárá; *Onire*, which is the Spirit of Iron who was the Chief of Onire; *Ògún Ikolẹ*, which is the Spirit of Iron who was the Chief of Ikolẹ; *Ògún Ẹlẹmonà*, which is the Spirit of Iron who was the Chief of Ẹlẹmonà; and *Ògún Akìrun* which is the Spirit of Iron who was the Chief of Akìrun. Each of these aspects of *Ògún* are preserved in the mythic tales of *Ògún* priests who served as chiefs in various regions of Yoruba culture.

Those *Ògún* worshippers in Africa who have a role in defending the community are called "*Ìjala Ògún*," and those *Ògún* worshippers in Africa who function as hunters are called

"*Ìrèmòjé Ògún.*" The overall community of *Ògún* worshippers is called "*Ègbè Ògún.*"

In some regions of Africa *Onilè*, who is the Owner of the Earth, is considered the female aspect of *Ògún*. Some areas of Africa consider *Onilè* a separate *Orisha* from *Ògún*, who has a close working relationship with him. In both instances the polarity between *Ògún and Onilè* is part of the *awo* (Mystery) associated with *Ogboni*. In traditional Yoruba culture, *Ogboni* is a council of elders who have both judicial and burial functions within the political and religious manifestations of *Ifá*.

In the West most *Ifá* and *Orisha* worshippers have a shrine for *Ògún* that is kept within the house, usually near the front door. In Africa it is more common to find a single shrine for *Ògún* at the entrance to the village that is used by the entire community. This is a tendency rather than a hard and fast rule.

IV.

ILẸ́ 'BORA
THE SHRINE OF THE SPIRIT OF IRON

A. *ILẸ́ 'BORA ADURA* Shrine for Prayer and Meditation to the Spirit of Iron

Western forms of *Orisha* worship generally place the shrine to *Ògún* near the front door of the house or apartment. Clearly this change in the location of the shrine is related to social conditions that exist in the West and it is one of many adaptations that has allowed *Ifá* and *Orisha* worship to survive in a new environment.

For those who have not received a consecrated *Ògún* pot from either and *Ifá* or an *Orisha* initiate, it is possible to make an altar for *Ògún* that can be used as a focal point for prayer and meditation. My recommendation is to take two railroad spikes and place them on a small mat near the front door of the residence. If this is not possible or convenient, it is acceptable to place the iron spikes in a wooden box. The box should be painted red and the inside of the box should be covered with some type of woven matting. If it is not possible to obtain a railroad spike, any nail or tool made from iron can be used instead.

Once you have selected the pieces of iron to be used, they should be rubbed with palm oil. While they are being rubbed, say a prayer to *Ògún* to protect your home and family. As you are going through the process of preparing the spikes, have a candle and a glass of water near the place where you are working. After the spikes have been covered with palm oil, cross them in the form of an X and either place them near the front door on a mat or inside the box.

Whenever you make prayers to *Ògún* sprinkle three drops of gin on the spikes, light a candle and say your prayer. Because this type of shrine is not consecrated, it is not appropriate to invoke *Ògún*. Instead make the following salutation:

Iba sẹ Ògún, mo juba.
I respect the Spirit of Iron and give Him praise.
Iba sẹ Ògún, mo juba.
I respect the Spirit of Iron and give Him Praise.
Iba sẹ Ògún, mo juba.
I respect the Spirit of Iron and give Him Praise.
Aṣẹ.
May it be so.

Prayers to *Ògún* should focus on concerns of both protection and removing obstacles from the process of spiritual growth. *Ògún* can also be approached in issues concerning truth, fair play and the resolution of disputes.

B. ILẸ́ 'BORA ORIKI — Shrine for Invocation to the Spirit of Iron

In most forms of *Orisha* worship in the West, a consecrated shrine to *Ògún* is made in a three-legged iron pot that is filled with iron tools and other ingredients that are sacred to *Ògún*. The exact process for making this type of shrine is taboo to the uninitiated.

Ògún worship in Africa is generally based on a five day cycle in which *Ògún* is invoked in front of his shrine every fifth day. Invocations to *Ògún* are called either *Oriki Ògún*, or *Ìjala Ògún*. The word "*Oriki*" means "praising the head," and the word "*Ìjala*" means "warrior guided by white cloth." The reference to white cloth is a symbolic expression of good character.

Ìjala Ògún is usually associated with martial skills and self-defense. These invocations are taught to those who are initiated in *Awo Ògún* (The Mystery of The Spirit of Iron) for use in specific ceremonial rites.

Oriki Ògún may be used by anyone who has received a consecrated *Ògún* pot. In *Ifá, Oriki Ògún* has certain key elements that may be shifted depending on the nature and content of the work that is being done. Some of these elements are as follows:

(Begin by offering praise to the mystery of the Spirit of Iron)

Iba sẹ Ògún awo, mo juba.
>I respect the Mystery of the Spirit of Iron and give Him Praise.

Iba sẹ Ògún awo, mo juba.
>I respect the Mystery of the Spirit of Iron and give Him Praise.

Iba sẹ Ògún awo, mo juba.
>I respect the Mystery of the Spirit of Iron and give Him Praise.

(The opening call is followed by acknowledgement of your individual road to *Ògún*, if this is unknown, all the roads of *Ògún* may be honored)

Iba sẹ Ògún Alárá, mo juba.
>I respect the Spirit of Iron who was the Chief of *Alara* and I give Him Praise.

Iba sẹ Ògún Onire, mo juba.
>I respect the Spirit of Iron who was the Chief of *Onire* and I give Him Praise.

Iba sẹ Ògún Ikolẹ, mo juba.
>I respect the Spirit of Iron who was the Chief of *Elemona* and I give Him Praise.

Iba sẹ Ògún Akìrun, mo juba.
>I respect the Spirit of Iron who was the Chief of *Akirun* and I give Him Praise.

Iba sẹ Ògún-un, mo juba.
>I respect the Spirit of Iron who is the guardian of those

who carve wood.

Iba sẹ Ògún oloola, mo juba.
> I respect the Spirit of Iron who is the guardian of those who perform circumcision.

(The opening greeting is followed by praise of the qualities of the Spirit of Iron, any or all of the following phrases may be used)

Ògún Olumaki, alaṣẹ o.
> Greetings to the Spirit of Iron, Chief of Strength, the Owner of Power.

Ògún oni 'rẹ.
> The Spirit of Iron is the Owner of the Mystery of Good Fortune.

Ògún alagere owo.
> The Spirit of Iron is the Owner of Abundance.

Ògún didẹ otun, Ògún didẹ osi.
> The Spirit of Iron.

Ògún abi-wow-gbogbogbo tii yo omo re nimu ofin ba mi.
> The Spirit of Iron who saves His children from destruction, save me.

(Make a request to have the Spirit of Iron remove obstacles from the path of Spiritual Growth)

Pa san ba pon ao lana to.
> Cut down the obstacles on the road.

Bi obi ba pon a lana to.
> When the kola nut ripens it opens the road.

Ni jo ti ma lana lati odẹ.
> Dancing outside opens the road.

(Offer thanks to the Spirit of Iron from providing blessings)

Eru Ògún ma mba mi o.
> I respect the Spirit of Iron for saving me.

Mo dupe Ògún onilẹ owo olona ola.
> I thank the Spirit of Iron who owns the House of
> Abundance and the road to Good Fortune

Ògún awo fun irẹ eda.
> The Mystery of the Spirit of Iron is for the good of all
> people.

Aṣẹ.
> May it be so.

C. *ADIMU ÒGÚN* — Offerings to the Spirit of Iron

In all forms of *Ifá* and *Orisha* worship it is traditional to make an offering whenever guidance or assistance is requested from Spiritual Forces. *Adimu* is a term that is generally used to refer to food and drink that is presented to the Spirit of a particular shrine. The idea behind the process of making an offering is that it would be unfair to ask for something for nothing.

One of the prayers that is used to make *adimu* offerings to *Ògún* is as follows:

Ògún (name of food) *rẹ rẹ o.*
> Spirit of Iron we give you (name of food).

Fun wa ni alafia.
> Grant us peace.

Ma pa wa o.
> Do not cause us harm.

Gba wa lowo iku.
> Protect us from Death.

Ma je k'omo de rẹ ewu oko.
> Protect our children from accidents.

Ògún aladaamẹji t'o mu bi ina.
> I pay homage to the Spirit of Iron because he is worthy
> of respect.

This prayer may be used in front of both a consecrated and an unconsecrated shrine.

D. *EBO ÒGÚN* — Life Force Offerings to the Spirit of Iron

The following offerings are given to the specific roads of *Ògún*. When *Ògún* receives dog, it is in those areas of Nigeria where dogs are a part of the rural diet.

1. *Ògún Alárá* — dog
2. *Ògún Onire* — ram
3. *Ògún Ikolẹ* — snail
4. *Ògún Ẹlẹ́monà* — roasted yams
5. *Ògún Akìrun* — the horns of a ram
6. *Ògún-un* — tree sap
7. *Ògún oloola* — snail

Whenever a life force offering is made to any of the *Orisha*, an invocation is made to *Ògún* as part of the process. This is a grossly misunderstood aspect of *Ifá* and *Orisha* worship which has suffered from negative stereotypes in the press and the general media. It is part of *awo Ògún* (Mystery of the Spirit of Iron) to learn the inner secrets of making life force offerings. Part of the process involves the elevation of the spirit of the animal into the land of the ancestors and the request that the spirit of the animal return to Earth to continue its role in providing nourishment to the community.

When an *Orisha* initiate is making a life force offering it should include an invocation for the *Odu Ògunda*. If the initiate is using the *Lucumi* system of *Merindinlogun*, the invocation would be to *Ògunda Meji*. In *Ifá* the invocation for life force offerings is to *Ògunda-Irẹtẹ*.

E. *AJÁBO ÒGÚN* — Charms for Protection with the Power of the Spirit of Iron

One of the aspects of *Ifá* and *Orisha* worship that is not well developed in the West is the use of *Ajábo* (charms) that are buried under the Earth. In Africa the construction of all *Orisha* and *Ifá* shrines involves the preparation of the ground itself. This usually

involves burying certain elements and herbs that attract the presence
of a particular Spiritual Force.

For those who want to provide additional protection to their
living area, take four iron spikes and some red and black yarn.
While sitting in front of *Ògún* with a glass of water and a lit
candle, rub the four spikes in palm oil. Take the black yarn and
wrap each spike. As you wrap each spike, say a prayer for those
things that you want kept away from your home. Start wrapping
the black thread from the top of the spike away from the direction
of your body. Then take the red yarn and wrap over the black yarn.
As you wrap each spike again say a prayer for those things that you
want kept away from your home. Start wrapping the red thread
from the bottom of the spike towards you.

After all the spikes are prepared, place them underground on
the four corners of your property. If this is not possible, place them
in the four outside corners of your house or apartment. The final
step is to ask *Ògún* to give you a clear sign when someone is
about to violate the taboos you have placed on your living space.
It is common in *Ifá* to have this sign be some physical reaction in
your body such as a tingling in the neck or an itching sensation on
the hand. Once this form of communication has been established
it is up to you to pay attention and take note of the warnings when
and if they come.

The art of making *ajábo* (charms) is very complex and
sophisticated within the various families of *Ògún* worshippers
throughout Africa. The charms themselves are called *ègbè*,
pęlu and *ayęta*.

V.

ÒGÚN ONI'RE
THE SPIRIT OF IRON AS THE
SOURCE OF GOOD FORTUNE

Ifá considers patience to be a blessing from the *Orisha*. According to *Ifá*, those who have patience may accomplish any task, may invoke for any form of abundance and are guaranteed a life of good fortune. In most instances when patience is suggested by divination as a solution to a particular problem, it is *Ògún* who is turned to for assistance. At the core of *Ògún aşę* (power) is the slow, steady willingness to do whatever it takes to complete a particular task.

Ògún clearing a path

VI.

ORIN ÒGÚN
SONGS TO THE SPIRIT OF IRON

A. **Call:** *Ògún dę aręrę ire gbogbo lokua, Ògún wanilę Ògún walona ire gbogbo lokua ę.*
    (Spirit of Iron come bring good fortune to greet each day, Spirit of Iron come to the house, Spirit of Iron come to the road and bring good fortune to greet each day.)
    Response: Repeat.

B. **Call:** *Sara ikoko Ògún dę Ògún Onilę.*
    Keep back, lift the Spirit of Iron's Pot, the Spirit of Iron and the Owner of the Earth.)
    Response: *Sara ikoko Onilę.*
    (Keep back, the Pot of the Owner of the Earth.)
    Call: *Ògún Onilę.*
    (The Spirit of Iron, the Owner of the Earth.)
    Response: *Sara ikoki Ògún dę.*
    (Keep back, lift the Spirit of Iron's Pot.)
    Call: *Ògún osa kuęlęyę.*
    (The power of the Spirit of Iron greets the surface of the Earth.)
    Response: *Sara ikoko Ògún dę.*
    (Keep back, lift the Spirit of Iron's Pot.)

C. **Call:** *Amala Ògún aręre amala ę a.*
    (Corn meal, the Spirit of Iron we praise you with corn meal.)
    Response: Repeat.
    Call: *Amala Ògún aręrę amala Okę.*
    (Corn meal, Spirit of Iron we praise you with corn meal from the mountain.)
    Response: Repeat.
    Call: *Ę afęręyo are afęręyo.*

(Protect us with your charm.)
Response: *Ẹ afẹrẹyo.*
(With your charm.)
Call: *Ẹ afẹrẹyo.*
(With your charm.)
Response: Repeat.
Call: *Arẹrẹ afẹrẹyo.*
(We praise your charm.)
Response: Repeat.
Call: *Ẹ afẹrẹyo.*
Response: Repeat.

Ògún's pot, and Ògún's spikes

ITEM #214
$8.95

HELPING YOURSELF WITH SELECTED PRAYERS

NOW OVER *130,000* IN PRINT!

The New Revised Helping Yourself with Selected Prayers provides an English translation for over 125 prayers of various religious beliefs. These prayers will provide a foundation upon which you can build your faith and beliefs. It is through this faith that your prayers will be fulfilled.

An index is provided to help the reader find the appropriate prayer for his or her particular request. The index also includes suggestions regarding the appropriate candle to burn while saying a particular prayer.

The devotions within these pages will help you pray consciously, vigorously, sincerely and honestly. True prayer can only come from within yourself.

ISBN 0-942272-01-3   5½"x 8½"   112 pages $8.95

ITEM #224
$6.95

Revised and Expanded

Success and Power Through Psalms

By Donna Rose

For thousands of years, men and women have found in the Psalms the perfect prayer book, possessing wisdom applicable to every human situation. Wise men and women of deep mystical insight have also learned to decipher the magical formulas David and the other Psalmists hid behind the written words. These formulas help the seeker solve everyday problems, achieve higher states of consciousness, gain material and spiritual wealth, as well as help defend himself or herself against psychic attacks and all manner of dangers.

The Revised and Expanded edition of Donna Rose's classic offers over 300 simple to perform magical rituals to help you manifest all of your desires using the magical powers of the psalms.

ISBN 0-942272-79-X 5½"x 8½ $6.95

New Revised

The Master Book of Candle Burning

How to Burn Candles for Every Purpose

POWERFUL
PSALM
RITUALS

HENRI GAMACHE

#043
$9.95

"How can I burn candles in a manner which will bring me the most satisfaction and consolation?"

In order to answer that question it is necessary to eliminate all technical, dry and often times torturous historical background. It is necessary to sift and sort every fact, scrutinize every detail, search for the kernel.

It is to be hoped that this volume answers that question in a manner which is satisfactory to the reader. It has been necessary, of course, to include some historical data and other anthropological data in order to better illustrate the symbolism involved in modern candle burning as practiced by so many people today.

This data has been accumulated from many sources: it has been culled from literally hundreds of books and articles. The modern rituals outlined here are based upon practices which have been described by mediums, spiritual advisors, evangelists, religious interpreters and others who should be in a position to know.

It has been the author's desire to interpret and explain the basic symbolism involved in a few typical exercises so that the reader may recognize this symbolism and proceed to develop his own symbolism in accordance with the great beauty and highest ethics of the Art.

ISBN 0-942272-56-0 5½"x 8½" $9.95

ITEM #053
$8.95

PAPA JIM'S
HERBAL MAGIC
WORKBOOK

Papa Jim is a very famous healer and root doctor. He brings you this compilation of remedies and potions from all over the world. Share the secret recipes that have mystically solved the problems of Papa Jim's many devotees. Learn how to unleash the magical powers of herbs.

Follow easy instructions on how to make
Herbal Baths, Mojo Bags, Sprinkling Powders,
Incenses and Teas for Love, Luck, Sex,
Money Drawing, Gambling
Protection, Hex Breaking, Jinx Removing and more!

Also incudes
English to Spanish / Spanish to English
translation for over 150 common herbs!

ISBN 0-942272-64-1 5½"x 8½" 112 pages $8.95